LITTLE TURTLE

ALLEN COUNTY PUBLIC LIBRARY

P9-EDX-609

J599.322
PORTER, KEITH. L 7115222
DISCOVERING RABBITS AND
 HARES

**DO NOT REMOVE
CARDS FROM POCKET**

**ALLEN COUNTY PUBLIC LIBRARY**

**FORT WAYNE, INDIANA 46802**

You may return this book to any agency, branch,
or bookmobile of the Allen County Public Library.

2-26-57

# Discovering

# RABBITS AND HARES

## Keith Porter

Illustrations by Wendy Meadway

The Bookwright Press
New York · 1986

# Discovering Nature

Allen County Public Library
Ft. Wayne, Indiana

**Discovering Bees and Wasps**
**Discovering Birds of Prey**
**Discovering Frogs and Toads**
**Discovering Rabbits and Hares**
**Discovering Snakes and Lizards**
**Discovering Spiders**
**Discovering Worms**

**Further titles are in preparation**

All photographs from Oxford Scientific Films

First published in the United States in 1986 by
The Bookwright Press
387 Park Avenue South
New York, NY 10016

First published in 1986 by
Wayland (Publishers) Limited
61 Western Road, Hove
East Sussex, BN3 1JD, England

©Copyright 1986 Wayland (Publishers) Limited

ISBN 0-531-18054-9

Library of Congress Catalog Card Number: 85-73665

Typeset by Planagraphic Typesetters Limited
Printed in Italy by G. Canale & C.S.p.A., Turin

# Contents

7115222

# Introducing Rabbits and Hares

## Origins and Relatives

Down in the meadow, just as the sun is rising, a whiskered snout sniffs the morning air. It belongs to a small furry animal with long ears, big eyes and strong back legs. It is of course a rabbit, an animal found almost all over the world.

The ancestors of the rabbit lived about 50 million years ago. We know this because bones and teeth of these early rabbit-like animals have been found in parts of Asia and North America. Since then many different types of rabbits and

**Below**  *A young rabbit out to feed.*

hares have **evolved**.

There are about forty different kinds of rabbits and hares in the world today. Almost half of them live in North America, a few live in Africa, and the rest live in Europe and Asia. They belong to a large group of animals called **mammals.**

In many ways rabbits look like mice or squirrels. They have bright eyes, long whiskers, and big front teeth. Unlike mice and squirrels, which are **rodents,** rabbits have short fluffy tails and fur-covered paws. Because of these and other

*This North American pika is a close relative of rabbits and hares.*

differences, the rabbits are placed in a group of their own, along with hares and small mouse-like animals called pikas.

Rabbits and hares are closely related to pikas. Over twelve kinds of pikas are known. Two kinds live in North America, and the rest live in Asia. Pikas look rather like guinea pigs with larger ears. In North America they are called rock rabbits or conies.

9

*Hares have much longer ears and legs than rabbits.*

## What Rabbits and Hares Look Like

Rabbits and hares have much the same body shape, although hares are usually bigger than rabbits, with longer legs and ears. All rabbits and hares have two different kinds of teeth. The large front ones are called chisel teeth, or **incisors.** The broad back ones are called cheek teeth, or **molars.**

The chisel teeth are used to bite off lengths of grass. The cheek teeth help to chop up or grind food. There is a wide gap between the chisel and cheek teeth. This is used to store food while nibbling.

The nose of a rabbit or a hare is very sensitive — it can smell much better than our noses. Inside each nostril is a special patch of skin called a sensory pad. These two pads are kept hidden under a fold of skin when the rabbit or hare is not sniffing the air. Rabbits and hares have long ears, which are sensitive to the slightest sound. Their large, round eyes give good, all-around vision.

**Above** *A close-up of a hare's nose showing its pads.*

The body of a rabbit or hare is covered with fur. This is made up of two kinds of hair. A soft type of hair, called underfur, lies next to the skin. This helps to keep the animal warm. In among the underfur are longer, tougher hairs. They give the fur its color. All rabbits and hares have a new coat of fur every year. They lose the old, long hairs and grow new ones. This is called **molting.**

The front feet of rabbits and hares have five toes, but the back feet have only four. Each toe ends in a sharp claw. The

*A rabbit with a mouthful of grass.*

rabbit's front claws are used for digging. Claws also help in fighting and for gripping the ground while running.

The feet of rabbits and hares have hairy soles. This helps them get a better grip on slippery rocks or ice. Most other animals have tough pads of skin on the soles of their feet.

11

# Where Rabbits and Hares Live

## Fields and Meadows

Rabbits and hares like to live in open grassy places. They can be found in fields and grassland all over the world. Hares make their home in open grassland but rabbits need somewhere to dig their burrows. Dry, sandy soils are best for digging in. But not all rabbits dig burrows; many **cottontails** live under bushes. Some rabbits live on banks or hillsides near fields, where the sloping ground helps to drain away water and keeps the burrows from flooding. They prefer small fields, surrounded by hedges, stone walls, or a border of trees, where they can run for shelter.

In some fields the hares and rabbits share their food with sheep and cows. In many fields the rabbits and hares feed on the grass and crops, often doing great

*A brown hare feeding in the evening. Hares travel a long way to find food.*

damage by eating the best plants.

Life in the fields can be dangerous, as there are many enemies about. Rabbits can dash to safety in their burrows, while hares usually escape from their enemies by running away quickly.

Almost all rabbits and hares are gray or brown colored. These dull colors help them to hide against their background. A brown animal, lying still in a field, is very difficult to see.

Rabbits and hares have not always lived in fields, because fields are made by people. Many thousands of years ago, most of the land was covered with trees. There were some wild, grassy places too. These large areas of grassland still exist in parts of the world today — they are called plains, prairies, savanna or steppes, according to the country in which they are found.

As people cut down the trees to make farmland, many rabbits and hares moved into the fields to live. Some still live in the wild grasslands or in woodland; others, like the American **jack rabbits,** which once lived in the open prairies, are now pests in the fields.

*A mother rabbit and two youngsters outside their warren. Some rabbits live on banks or hillsides near fields.*

## Arctic and Mountain Life

A few rabbits and hares live in cold parts of the world. The Arctic hare lives in northern Europe and North America. The very similar snowshoe hare is found only in North America.

Both of these hares have a way of disguising themselves at different times of year. As winter comes they molt, changing their brownish fur to a white coat.

**Below** *You have to look carefully to see the snowshoe hare in this picture.*

*This type of Arctic landscape is home to many hares.*

This helps them to hide when the winter snows cover the ground.

The snowshoe hare is very good at running across soft snow. In winter it grows long, thick hairs on its feet. Like snowshoes, they help to spread the hare's weight on the soft snow. Both snowshoe hares and Arctic hares dig burrows to reach plants buried under the snow.

Hairy feet and wide toes help the snowshoe and Arctic hares run on slippery ice. They can run just as fast over ice as over rough ground. Farther south the snowshoe hare and the Arctic hare live on high mountains. Some other rabbits and hares also live on mountains. The woolly hare lives as high as 5,000 meters (16,400 feet) in the Himalayas. Its fur is silver-gray all year round and its coat is thick and woolly to keep out the cold. Mountains are very cold places to live.

The volcano rabbit is an unusual rabbit. It lives as high as 4,000 meters (13,100 feet) on the slopes of some Mexican volcanoes. It is the smallest rabbit at just over 34 cm (13 inches) long. It is unusual in not having a tail.

15

## Deserts, Swamps and Forests

Some rabbits and hares live in unusual places. The black-tailed jack rabbit (a hare) survives in hot, dry deserts; the North American swamp and marsh rabbits both live in wet places, and, in some parts of the world, rabbits live in forests.

Desert hares and rabbits come out only at night in order to avoid the hot daytime. Some desert cottontails spend the day in burrows made by other animals. The hares hide in the shade or dig shallow holes in the ground.

Like many desert-living animals, the black-tailed jack rabbit has huge ears.

These are used to control the animal's temperature. When the hare is hot it can lose heat from the large surface area of its ears. At night-time it can cut down the amount of blood flowing through the skin of its ears. This helps it to keep warm in the cold desert nights.

Some African hares live in dry, grassy places. The red rock hares spend the day in "dens" among the rocks. They sometimes block the entrance to the den with piles of sticks.

**Below**  *The mottled coat of this Cape hare is the same color as its surroundings, which helps it to hide from enemies.*

Swamp and marsh rabbits are large relatives of cottontails. In marshy places, a burrow would soon fill with water. So, instead of making burrows, these rabbits live among the grasses near pools. They are very good swimmers.

A few hares and rabbits live in forests.

*An American marsh rabbit.*

They do not dig burrows, but shelter among the trees and bushes, or in holes in the ground. The tropical forests of South America and Sumatra are both places in which forest rabbits live.

# Family Life

## Space for Living and Feeding

All animals need space in which to live. In this space they feed and bring up a family. Such spaces are called territories.

Rabbits live in groups. Each rabbit digs a burrow near its neighbors. Lots of burrows connected together are called a **warren.** A warren can cover a whole hillside and may be made up of many territories.

Female rabbits, or **does,** often share a large feeding territory. Within this area they eat side by side. A doe with a family may set up her own small territory. This is usually near the burrow where she brings up her family. The best territories

*A warren with a section cut away to show the network of tunnels.*

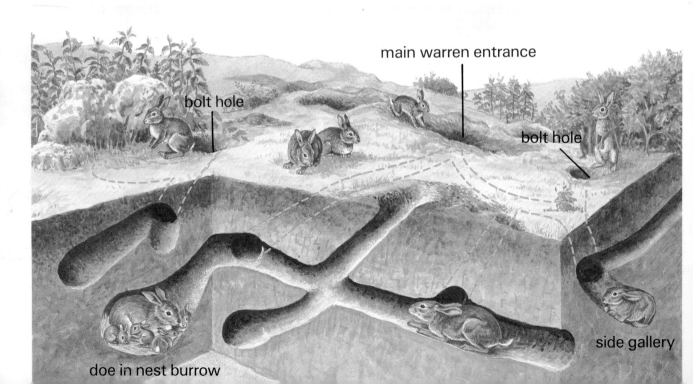

main warren entrance

bolt hole

bolt hole

side gallery

doe in nest burrow

*A buck rabbit "chinning" to mark the ground with his scent.*

have the most food.

Male rabbits, or **bucks,** have larger territories than those of does. Each buck rabbit "guards" several does. He keeps intruders out by marking his territory with special scents. A buck produces one of these scents from among the fur under his chin. He rubs his chin against the ground or on plants. Buck rabbits also leave their scent by squirting urine.

The larger a buck's territory, the more does he can mate with. Bucks fight viciously over their territories and old buck rabbits often have many scars from such fights.

During the day, rabbits rest in their burrows, while hares hide in the grass. Hares do not live in large family groups and they do not use burrows as "nurseries." Most hares have very large territories. They live alone and wander many miles to feed. During the day, they hide by lying in hollows in the ground. These hiding places are called **forms,** and are usually in tall grass or under bushes.

## Rabbit Courtship and Mating

The mother rabbit is the center of family life. She can **mate** with a buck and produce babies when she is only a few months old. Most kinds of rabbits give birth to up to eight babies. They are called a **litter**. Some rabbits can have five or more litters in one year.

*A male and female rabbit playing together. This is part of their courtship.*

Each buck may mate with several does. Before mating, the buck and doe go through various stages of chasing and feeding. This is called courtship.

During courtship the buck chases the doe until she stops. The buck may then hop around her, with his tail bent over to show his white fur. When she is ready, the doe lets the buck climb on to her back and mate with her.

Twenty-eight days after mating, the doe will give birth to her babies. Before

that she has to prepare a special nursery burrow, or breeding stop. This is a short tunnel with only one entrance. At the end of this tunnel the doe collects pieces of grass and moss to make a nest. She pulls out some of her own belly fur to make a soft, warm lining.

Older does often make their nests in a part of the main warren. If the ground is nice and soft, younger does usually dig

*A doe collects grass which she will use to make her nest.*

their breeding stops some distance away from the warren.

As the time draws near for the babies to be born, the doe will chase other rabbits out of her burrow. She continues to defend her burrow until the young rabbits are ready to look after themselves.

## The Family Life of the Rabbit

New born rabbits (called kits or kittens) are blind and deaf. They have almost no fur and cannot move their legs. They grow very quickly on their mother's milk. This is a very rich food and gives the baby rabbits all they need. The mother comes to feed her babies only once each day, for about five minutes. Between times the doe closes the burrow entrance with soil to keep other animals

*Newborn rabbits are blind and helpless.*

(even other rabbits) from eating her babies.

At ten days old the kits open their eyes. By sixteen days old they can eat grass. At three weeks old they start to explore outside the nest but still come back to take milk from the doe.

The young rabbits can look after themselves at one month old. But the outside world is full of dangers. Many baby rabbits are killed by **predators**; others die from disease, or from cold and starvation during the winter. Over half

*At ten days old, a baby rabbit's eyes have just opened.*

*When they are three or four weeks old, baby rabbits leave their nest to feed outside.*

the total number of baby rabbits die before they are six months old and very few wild rabbits live longer than a year. A pet rabbit, however, can live for twelve or thirteen years.

The doe continues to breed throughout the summer and into the autumn. By the end of the year she may have "grandchildren" as her first babies of the year begin to breed.

23

## The Family Life of the Hare

Hares often come together in groups during the breeding season. The male hares, also called "jacks," sometimes box with each other. These fights test their strength and help each female or "jill" to choose a strong, healthy mate. Sometimes these boxing matches are between a jack and a jill. It is part of their courtship play. The strongest jack will mate with several jills. Six weeks after mating, the jill gives birth to her babies.

Baby hares are called **leverets.** They are born above ground, in the mother

*A jack and jill boxing. These mock fights form part of their courtship.*

*At a few hours old these baby hares can already run around.*

*A leveret waits in its form for its mother to come and feed it.*

hare's form. Baby hares are very different from baby rabbits. They are born with fur and with their eyes open. Within an hour they can even run around. Their fur helps them keep warm in the open fields.

Each mother hare produces between two and four babies in a litter. There are usually three or four litters in a year, although some hares can produce up to six in one year.

After about three days the mother hare splits up her litter. She takes each baby to its own special form. Before leaving, she may cover each baby with some grass to help hide it. The mother visits her babies once each day, to feed them on milk. Some hares feed each leveret separately. Other hares have a special feeding place where all the leverets gather. The leverets leave their forms at sunset to meet up with their brothers and sisters. The jill feeds each one on milk for a few minutes. The leverets then hop back to the safety of their forms for another day.

Baby hares grow very quickly. After a week or so they can eat grass. By the time they are a month old they can look after themselves.

# Staying Alive

## Food and Feeding

All rabbits and hares eat plants, grass being one of their favorite foods. On farmland they are attracted to crops; fields of grain, lettuces, or carrots are very popular.

In winter, when food is scarce, rabbits and hares feed on roots, berries or bark, and in woodlands they may pull down any small twigs they can reach. Now and again they will also eat snails, worms, and other small animals.

Rabbits and hares feed mainly at night. They come out in the evening. Later, as the sun rises, they begin to creep back into their hiding places. However, in very quiet places, rabbits and hares sometimes feed during the day.

*This rabbit has found a field full of wheat to feast on.*

26

Rabbits and hares have a very strange way of digesting food. They actually eat the same food twice over, and they do this by producing two kinds of droppings.

In the daytime, when they are not sleeping, they produce their first droppings. These are soft pellets containing pieces of undigested plants and tiny organisms called bacteria. The bacteria help to digest the food and get all the goodness

Small, dry pellets like these, and damaged trees, are sure signs that rabbits live nearby.

**Below** *A rabbit swallows its first soft pellets to extract more goodness from the food it has eaten.*

out. The rabbit or hare eats these soft pellets as soon as they are pushed out of the body. The pellets are then digested a second time and the full goodness is absorbed.

In the evening, when the rabbit or hare comes out to feed, it produces dry, brown pellets. These contain the waste parts of plants. They are a tell-tale sign that rabbits or hares live nearby.

## Enemies of Rabbits and Hares

Many animals eat rabbits and hares. Foxes, wolves and coyotes catch them above ground, while rats, weasels and stoats attack the babies, and chase rabbits down their burrows. Eagles, hawks and buzzards hunt them from the air.

Most rabbits and hares are easily caught by their predators, although some larger rabbits and hares will fight back. Hares will chase off snakes, which try to take their leverets, and rabbits sometimes use their back legs to kick and attack smaller enemies, such as weasels and stoats.

Rabbits and hares are very wary when feeding. A group of rabbits often post a "lookout." This guard rabbit sits up on its back legs on an ant hill or tree stump.

*A rabbit on the alert for any signs of danger.*

If it sees or hears an enemy it will sound the alarm. It tells other rabbits to scoot into their burrows by thumping on the ground with its back legs.

Running rabbits and hares also give a warning. Most of them have white undersides to their tails. As they run from danger their tails bob up and down to show a flash of white. This acts as a danger signal to all rabbits or hares nearby.

The white-sided jack rabbit has an amazing warning signal. It has a brown back and white sides. If it senses danger, the white fur can be pulled over onto its back. In bright sunlight it can "flash" a signal to all other jack rabbits nearby.

Most hares escape their enemies by running very fast. The white-sided jack rabbit can outrun even a fox or a coyote.

*A fox drags away its kill, a rabbit, to eat.*

## Parasites and Diseases

All animals have smaller animals living on or inside their bodies. These are called **parasites.** Rabbits and hares have quite a few parasites. Inside they are infected with many different kinds of worms, while bloodsucking fleas, ticks and lice live outside, on the skin. These parasites do not usually do much harm, although a lot of parasites in a single rabbit or hare may weaken it and even kill it.

Like all animals, rabbits and hares suffer from diseases. Disease is most common in rabbits when they live in small, crowded warrens. Disease can also strike if food is scarce and the rabbits or hares are weak.

The best known disease of rabbits is called myxomatosis. This is caused by a tiny organism called a **virus**. The human common cold is also caused by a virus.

The myxomatosis virus is common in the South American forest rabbit. However, it does not do much harm to this rabbit. But in 1897 myxomatosis was found to kill the European rabbit when the disease spread from wild forest rabbits to some pet rabbits in South America.

In some parts of the world, myxomatosis is spread by the rabbit flea. All fleas drink blood. They pick up the virus from a rabbit already sick with myxomatosis. The fleas then feed on another, healthy, rabbit and the virus enters the

*A rabbit with myxomatosis. This disease can kill a rabbit in twelve days.*

new rabbit's bloodstream.

A rabbit with myxomatosis looks horrible. Its eyelids swell until it cannot see; its head swells up and it becomes deaf. The virus can kill the rabbit 12 days after infecting it. Myxomatosis only kills the

*A flea feeding on a rabbit's ear. This is how rabbits become infected with the disease myxomatosis.*

European rabbit; it does not harm other rabbits or hares.

31

# Rabbits and People

## The Spread of the European Rabbit and Hare

The European rabbit is found all over the world. It once lived only in Mediterranean countries. The Romans ate rabbits and hares. They kept them in walled gardens. As the Romans conquered various countries they took the rabbit with them. In this way rabbits soon spread to Spain, France, and Germany.

The rabbit was brought to Britain by the Normans. Some were let loose on small islands. Here they could breed but not escape. Others were kept in large enclosures called warrens (we now use

*A medieval rabbit warren. Dogs were used to chase rabbits from their burrows to be caught and killed for the pot.*

this name for a group of rabbit burrows). Rabbits are good at escaping and many soon dug, or jumped, their way out of these enclosures and spread over much of the countryside.

The European rabbit grows very quickly. It also produces lots of babies. For these reasons many rabbits were taken on sailing ships, to be used as fresh meat by the sailors. Rabbits were set free on islands all over the world. They bred there and provided meat for sailors who stopped by in passing ships.

During the nineteenth century, Euro-

*A nineteenth-century warrener and his dogs at work.*

pean settlers took rabbits to Australia, New Zealand and South America, where they wanted to be able to shoot and eat them. Unfortunately, the rabbits soon became pests in these countries.

The European hare was also taken to other countries, including Australia, New Zealand and South America. It is now a pest in many places, and huge numbers of hares are caught every year. Some are even imported as meat to Europe.

33

## Rabbits and Hares as Pests

Much of the world's land is now farmed. The farmers plow the soil and grow various crops, such as rice, wheat, corn, and vegetables, for human food. Other crops are planted for different reasons: fields of grass are grown for cattle; trees are grown to produce wood; clover and alfalfa are grown to keep the soil rich and to provide animal fodder.

Many of these crops can be badly damaged by rabbits and hares. Farmland is a paradise for them. Here there is plenty of food and the animals can find shelter in the hedges which are often planted around the edges of the fields.

Many hares live in among the crops. They move into fields once the plants are tall enough to hide them. Mountain hares come down to feed on crops in winter.

Rabbits usually live outside or around the edges of fields. They sneak into the grass or crops in the evening, and feed

*The brown patches in this field of wheat show where rabbits and hares have been grazing.*

*A North American black-tailed jack rabbit.*

close to their burrows along the edges of the fields.

With so much food around, many rabbits and hares breed quickly. They soon become pests. In Australia, during the early part of this century, the rabbits ate so much grass that sheep starved to death. They also turned green fields into deserts by eating all the plants. Rabbits and hares can also be a nuisance in pastureland, because they eat the best grass before the sheep or cattle can get to it.

In the United States the black-tailed jack rabbit is one of the farmer's greatest enemies. It feeds on the young shoots in wheat and corn fields.

Some rabbits and hares eat parts of trees. They usually do this in winter when food is scarce. The snowshoe hare feeds almost entirely on tree bark in winter, and kills, or damages, large numbers of small trees.

## Controlling Numbers

Rabbits and hares breed very quickly and, when their numbers build up, they can do a lot of damage to crops. All over the world, farmers occasionally have to wage war on these animals.

There are several different ways of controlling rabbits and hares. Small areas of trees and gardens can be protected by a fence. This is partly buried in the ground to stop rabbits from burrowing under it. However, fencing costs a lot of money, so it is not often used. Usually, the animals are killed, either by shooting, trapping and snaring, or by gassing rabbits when they are in their burrows.

In open fields, hares can be chased into fenced areas and then killed. These chases or "rabbit drives," take place a lot in western areas of North America, where hares can be a serious pest.

Rabbits are easier to catch than hares. Nets can be placed over the entrance holes to their burrows. Each hole is then filled

*When young trees are planted their trunks can be protected from nibbling rabbits by a plastic tube.*

with smoke or poison and the escaping rabbits are caught in the nets.

Another common way of catching rabbits is to put ferrets down their burrows. Ferrets are small weasel-like animals. They will chase rabbits and scare them out of their burrows. The Romans used ferrets to catch wild rabbits many hundreds of years ago.

In 1951 a new way of controlling the European rabbit was discovered. The disease myxomatosis was deliberately brought, by some farmers, to parts of Europe and Australia. It soon spread, killing millions of rabbits.

Many people thought it was a horrible way to kill rabbits. Even so, it has helped many farmers in Europe and Australia. Most rabbits today are resistant to the myxomatosis virus, but a few still die every year in local outbreaks of the disease.

*After a ferret is put down a burrow, nets are placed over the openings to catch the rabbits as they run out.*

# Learning More About Rabbits and Hares

**In the Wild**

Rabbits feed mainly in the late evening or early morning when the dim light hides them from their enemies. The wild rabbit or hare is always alert and watching for the sly fox or the slinking weasel. To see wild rabbits or hares we must first find out where they live.

Look for the signs left behind by rabbits that have been feeding on sand dunes, hillsides, or the edges of fields and woods. They leave piles of bare

*This little girl has found a nest of baby cottontails in her yard.*

*Hares are not easy to find in the wild. This young one hides by crouching in the grass.*

earth around their warrens. You can tell if a warren is being used by looking for small round droppings, closely nibbled grass and other chewed plants.

To watch rabbits you need to find a place with a good view of the warren but somewhere that keeps you hidden. This may mean sitting quietly under a tree or behind a hedge.

Hares are not as easy to see because they usually live alone and leave very few signs. The most likely places to find them are in open grassy fields on farmland. If you look in the early morning or evening, you may be lucky and see one before it leaps away through the long grass.

If you are really lucky you may find a baby hare, or leveret, hidden in the grass. You must remember that it has probably been hidden by its mother, so be careful not to touch it or frighten it away. If you do she may not be able to find it again.

## Rabbits as Pets

People keep rabbits for many reasons. Not long ago most were kept for eating and they still are today in some countries. Rabbits are also bred for their fur.

Today many children keep rabbits as pets. They are easy to keep and most live happily out of doors. But some rabbits are not as tough as their wild cousins; they need protection from the cold and from drafts.

Almost all pet rabbits are kept in hutches. These are usually long wooden boxes on legs. They have two parts, each with a door. One half is used as a ''bedroom'' and contains clean hay to let the rabbit snuggle down. The other half has a wire front and is where the rabbit eats its food.

Besides a hutch, the rabbit needs somewhere to run around. This can be a fenced off part of the yard. Without a fence the rabbit would soon escape.

Rabbits spend a lot of time eating. All

*You can buy this kind of rabbit hutch in most pet shops, or make one yourself.*

pet shops sell special types of rabbit food. Rabbits need clean hay to eat, and green plants are also important in their diet. Almost all vegetables and wild plants are eaten by rabbits.

Unless you want to breed rabbits, the does and bucks must be kept apart. Two

*A triangular run gives a pet rabbit lots of room to exercise. As the grass is eaten, the run can be moved to a fresh patch.*

rabbits can quickly become twenty-two rabbits. If looked after properly, rabbits can live for twelve years or more.

## Domestic Breeds of Rabbits

All animals produce strange individuals now and again. Some are white animals called albinos, others may be black. Rabbit breeders like to keep and breed unusual rabbits. They may even try to breed their own varieties. Over 90 different types, or breeds, of pet rabbits are now known. All come from the wild European rabbit.

Some breeds are kept for their unusual fur. The chinchilla rabbit is bred on huge farms. It has a very soft, deep fur,which is used to make fur coats.

The angora rabbit has been kept for hundreds of years for its long fur. This is used to make a soft, fluffy wool. Some angora rabbits look more like small

**Below** *White rabbits are among the most common domestic breeds.*

*A lop-eared rabbit in its hutch.*

sheep than rabbits.

The largest breed is called the Flemish giant. This is a huge rabbit, weighing about 7½ kilos (16½ pounds). It is kept mainly for meat.

Most rabbits have been bred as exhibition animals. They come in many shapes and colors. Black rabbits and pure white breeds are probably the most common. A few have unusually colored fur. The Bevern rabbit has pale blue fur, while the harlequin has light and dark patches, like a chess board.

The strangest of all are the lop-eared rabbits. They have huge, floppy ears, which may be 60 cm (24 inches) long. These rabbits look nothing like their ancestors, the wild rabbits.

# Glossary

**Buck** The male of various animals, including rabbits and hares.

**Cottontail** The name given to several kinds of rabbit found in North America.

**Doe** The female of various animals, including rabbits and hares.

**Evolved** Developed gradually — the way animals and plants have changed through the years to adapt to conditions on earth.

**Form** The special hiding place of a hare, made in a shallow hollow on the ground, usually in the grass.

**Incisors** Long, front, cutting teeth which are shaped like chisels.

**Jack rabbit** The name given to several kinds of North American hare.

**Leveret** A baby hare.

**Litter** A group of baby animals, born at the same time, from the same mother.

**Mammals** Warm-blooded animals, with hair or fur, which feed their babies on milk.

**Mate** To come together for breeding. Male and female animals mate to produce young.

**Molars** Broad, flat, back teeth which are used for chewing and grinding food.

**Molting** Losing an old coat of fur and growing a new one in its place. The coat molts gradually so as not to leave the animal bare.

**Parasite** A small animal that lives and feeds on or inside the body of a larger animal.

**Predator** An animal that hunts and kills other animals for food.

**Rodents** A group of mammals, including mice, rats, beavers and squirrels, all of which have large, front teeth for gnawing.

**Virus** A tiny organism, which can be seen only with a powerful microscope. Viruses can only live inside animals and plants. They often cause disease.

**Warren** The home of a group of rabbits; an underground network of burrows.

# Finding Out More

If you would like to find out more about rabbits and hares you might read the following books:

Bare, Colleen S. *Rabbits and Hares.* New York: Dodd, Mead, 1983.

Henrie, Fiona. *Rabbits.* New York: Franklin Watts, 1980.

Silverstein, Alvin and Virginia Silverstein. *Rabbits: All About Them.* New York: Lothrop, 1973.

Steinberg, Phil. *You and Your Pet: Rodents and Rabbits.* Minneapolis: Lerner Publications, 1978.

# Index

## Picture Acknowledgments

Survival Anglia — T. Andrewartha 25 (left); J. and D. Bartlett 16; J. Foott 14, 35. All other photographs from Oxford Scientific Films by the following photographers: G.I. Bernard cover, opp. title page, 8, 11, 19, 20, 21, 22, 23, 25 (right), 26, 27, 28, 29, 30, 31, 34, 36, 37, 39; J. Dermid 17, 38; M.P.L. Fogden 9, 10; A. Holley 24; C. Houghton 13; R. Kamal 42; R. Packwood 12; Dr. R. Parks 15; A. Ramage 41, 43. Artwork by Wendy Meadway.